Creative Gift Wrapping

fun, quick & easy projects

Contributing Writer
Nancy Wall Hopkins

PUBLICATIONS INTERNATIONAL, LTD.

Louis Weber, C.E.O.
Publications, International, Ltd.
7373 North Cicero Avenue
Lincolnwood, Illinois 60646

Manufactured in USA.

8 7 6 5 4 3 2 1

ISBN 0-7853-0339-1

Nancy Wall Hopkins is a writer and stylist for a number of national publications and books. She frequently works on package design.

Photography by Sam Griffith Studio, Inc.

Model: Pamela Kaplanes/Royal Model Management

CONTENTS

INTRODUCTION

It's been said there's only one chance to make a first impression. And when it comes to gift wrapping, first impressions are everything. In fact, how a package looks on the outside sets the tone for the gift inside. After all, even the most wonderful gifts seem inadequate when presented in a shabby wrapping with little attention paid to small—but special—details. On the other hand, a gift that is beautifully wrapped in splendid paper and topped with a shimmery ribbon can turn the simplest gift into a grand present. A splendidly wrapped package illustrates the love and care that went into the selection of a gift. Whether it's taking the time to select the perfect ribbon in the recipient's favorite color, hand stenciling a whimsical paper, or creating a child-pleasing name tag—what could be more fun than giving a gift wrapped from the heart?

The 40 designs in this book have been created with all of your special wrapping needs in mind. There are ideas for traditional holidays such as Christmas, Valentine's Day, Mother's Day, Father's Day, and Halloween. Also included are ideas for other gift-giving occasions like promotions, moving days, and leaving the nest. There are irresistible wraps for birthdays and once-in-a-lifetime wedding days, anniversaries, and graduations. You'll also find quick wraps for when your schedule is tight, fun wraps for times when the kids want to lend a hand, and extraordinary wraps for those occasions when only the best will do. Some are so beautiful that the recipient will reuse them and treasure them long after the gift is gone. You'll even find great wrap-ups for housewarming and hostess gifts, as well as inspired ideas for difficult-to-wrap money and bottles.

Most importantly, the ideas in this book are simple, requiring a minimum of effort and skill. A special "Basic Wrap" section guarantees a perfect, failproof wrap every time. Easy-to-follow steps and how-to photographs carefully guide you through the wrapping of each package. You'll find tips for creating a springy cardboard basket, wrapping a box in fancy and casual fabrics, and covering a box in satiny ribbons. Better yet are the ideas that don't even rely on a box. How about colorful, always available bags, bandannas, baskets, and buckets?

Many of the packages featured rely on a few equipment basics: a pair of scissors, double-sided tape or glue, and a sturdy ruler. Others require a few extras such as acrylic paints, brushes, sponges, markers, stencil patterns, etc. Even though most of the items used for gift wrapping are easily available in your own home, a handy source list will help you locate any hard-to-find items.

All of the packages can be easily adapted to fit a variety of occasions or personalized for your very special recipient. Be sure to check out the helpful hints for additional wrapping options. With this special guide, you'll really become a gift wrapping expert.

PAPER POINTERS

When choosing the perfect wrapping paper, it's wise to remember that papers, just like people, have personalities all their own. However, there's more to selecting an appropriate wrapping paper than matching the recipient's personality. You must also consider why you are giving the gift. Is it a special occasion, birthday, or holiday? Once you've pinpointed the reason, consider the season. Generally, light and breezy pastel papers work best in the spring, while rich, boldly hued wrapping papers are favored during the winter months. Lastly, what are the characteristics of the gift? What size and shape is it? Does it have a specific use? Most small gifts look terrific when wrapped in delicate prints and solids—papers that do not overwhelm the package. Large packages hold their own quite well in noisy prints, geometrics, and bold stripes.

Today, choosing the perfect paper is not limited to traditional wrapping papers. Take a look at winning options such as versatile cellophane, brilliant mylar, interesting scraps of fabric, lacy doilies, handmade marbled and textured papers, newspaper pages, pearlized tissue papers, sturdy wallpaper, scented drawer liners . . . even bandannas, scarves, and ribbons! Let your creativity take charge as you explore the wonderful options!

IT'S A WRAP
BASIC WRAP
DIRECTIONS

While the possibilities for a winning wrap are virtually endless, it's nice to know one failproof, quick and easy wrapping technique that works every time. To get started, first decide how much paper you'll need using the following formulas:

Paper Length = (2 × Box Width) + (2 × Box Height) + 2

Paper Width = Box Length + Box Height + 2

For example, for a basic shirt box measuring $11\frac{1}{2}$ (l) × $8\frac{1}{2}$ (w) × $1\frac{1}{2}$ (h) inches, you will need a 22- × 15-inch sheet of wrapping paper. For a square box measuring 7 × 7 × 7 inches, you will need a 30- × 16-inch sheet. If you're wrapping a box with slightly different measurements than those contained in this book, don't be discouraged. Simply adjust the sizes to fit your box. Once you've determined how much paper to cut, rely on these four quick-and-easy steps to make the rest a cinch!

1. Place the sheet of wrapping paper on a work surface. Center the box, wrong-side up, on the wrapping paper so that the long side of the box runs parallel to the short side of the paper. Working with the long side of the box facing forward, bring the bottom edge of the paper toward the center of the box. Secure with double-sided tape.

2. Fold down the top edge of the paper ½ inch. Place a length of tape along the fold. Bring the folded top portion toward the center of the box, pressing the taped fold firmly against the box to seal.

3. To wrap the ends, fold the sides of the paper in toward the center so that the paper forms triangular flaps at the top and bottom of the box. Press along the folds firmly to crease. Fold the top triangle down toward the center of the box, pressing firmly. Secure with double-sided tape.

4. Fold the bottom triangle up toward the center of the box, pressing firmly and overlapping the top triangle. Fold down the top triangle ½ inch. Secure the folded triangle with double-sided tape. Repeat on the opposite end of the package. Turn the package right-side up.

DON'T WRAP IT!

Sometimes, traditional wrapping techniques just do not work. How do you wrap a puppy, potted tree, or car? The best advice is not to. A gigantic or living gift that is simply ribboned and topped with a huge triple bow is far more appealing than one that's stuffed into a garbage bag or wrapped in a giant jumble of pieced papers. Instead of disguising such a gift, play it up. For example, beribbon that lovely potted tree that your friend wanted so much for her house. Do the same for that cuddly puppy—the cold nose and friendly eyes will do the rest.

When large gifts are of a more manageable size, you can rely on extra large iridescent or decorative plastic bags available at party and stationery stores. They're very convenient and look great when bundled and tied with a brilliant bow.

RIBBON REGALIA

Every well-wrapped package looks so much better when it is topped with a perky ribbon. It's the ideal finishing touch. And when it comes to choosing the perfect ribbon— whether plain or fancy, feminine or masculine, serious or silly—there's always a ribbon that's right for your wrapping needs! Take a look at the varied options offered by today's party, craft, and stationery stores. These days, ribbon possibilities are endless. There are lavish wire-edged ribbons, simple cords, raffia, and strings; rich silk, moire, and taffeta ribbons; cheery curling ribbons; versatile cotton, metallic, and mylar ribbons; and functional waterproof ribbons. By the spool or by the yard in every width and color imaginable, many stores offer a vast selection of ready-made ribbons in all shapes and sizes. You'll also find that fabric stores offer a winning collection of yarns, braids, cords, woven laces, and ribbons, not to mention decorative buttons, tassels, buckles, and trims. Just about any adornment can be a fitting final touch to a gift!

BOW BASICS

Once wrapped, one of the simplest ways to lend a finishing flourish is to top your gift with a brilliant, sumptuously tied bow. Difficult to make as they sometimes appear, tying a beautiful bow is as easy as tying your shoe! It's a matter of building on the basics. Here's how it works.

To create a double bow, first place an appropriate length (generally (2 × Box Width) + (2 × Box Height)) of the ribbon under the box with equal ends extending. Bring the ends together at the center and tie them into a single knot. Pass the end of a second length of ribbon (1 to 1½ yards) under the knot. Bring the ends together and tie them into a bow over the knot. To make a double bow, pass a second length (1 to 1½ yards) of ribbon under the first bow. Bring the ends together once again at the center and tie the second length into a bow over the knot of the first bow. To make a triple or a quadruple bow, simply repeat again using a third or fourth length of ribbon of the same length.

MAKING YOUR OWN

There's absolutely no limit to the number of elegant packages you can create when you rely on store-bought wrapping papers. But presenting an extraordinary package wrapped in a pretty paper that you created yourself adds to the enjoyment of both giving and receiving. Whether it's a whimsically sponged, stamped, or stenciled paper for the kids or an elegantly drizzled and painted paper for that once-in-a-lifetime occasion, there's a fun and easy technique to suit your gift-giving needs. Check out your local craft, party, or stationery stores for a great selection of ready-to-use stamps, stencils, paints, and craft sponges.

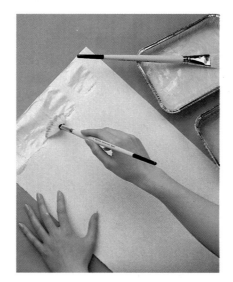

Although ready-made craft sponges are available in a variety of shapes and sizes, you can easily create your own pleasing designs. It's as easy as 1-2-3.

1. Draw your design onto tracing paper or plain white paper. Cut out the design and place it on a dry sponge. (For best results, choose a sponge with tiny holes.)
2. Using a pen or felt-tip marker, trace the design onto the sponge.
3. Cut out the design with sharp scissors and you're set.

PRESENTS BY MAIL

A beautifully wrapped present lovingly sent by mail brings immeasurable pleasure to its lucky recipient. To make sure your package arrives in mint condition, review the handy checklist below.

■ If the gift you're planning to mail is especially fragile, first wrap it in protective bubble paper available at packaging stores before you wrap it in paper. Place the gift in the gift box and fill all around the gift with protective loose fill or plastic foam peanuts, shredded tissue, or straw. Then wrap the box as desired.

■ Make sure the mailing box you're planning to use is sturdy and stable. The box should provide ample space all around the gift for a protective packing material, such as loose fill, plastic foam peanuts, shredded tissue, or straw.

■ Fill the bottom of the mailing box with protective packing material.

■ Overwrap the wrapped gift in a protective plastic bag. This keeps the packing material from becoming entangled in the bow or decorative adornment and allows the recipient to easily lift the gift from the box. In addition, the plastic covering protects the gift in case the box should become damaged by water while in transit. You can use a cooking bag for small packages; a small trash bag works well for large packages.

■ Place the gift in the mailing box. Add additional packing material to secure the gift on all sides.

■ Tape the box shut using box sealing tape suitable for mailing.

■ Properly label the gift, double checking names and addresses. Be sure to mark food and fragile gifts properly. Consult your local packaging store if you have questions regarding the best way to wrap and send a perishable gift.

GIFT WRAPPING RESOURCES

The Box Shoppe
Weed Street Center
1001 W. North Avenue
Chicago, IL 60622
312-915-5995

This store offers a complete range of gift and specialty boxes, including folding boxes, two-piece apparel boxes, jewelry boxes, and mailing boxes in a wide variety of shapes and sizes. The Box Shoppe will ship boxes across the country.

C.M. Offray and Son, Inc.
P.O. Box 601 Route 24
Chester, NJ 07930
Attention: Customer Service
1-800-344-5533

A comprehensive range of top-quality "Woven-Edge Ribbons and Arts, Crafts, Gifts & Floral Ribbons™" available at fabric and notion stores from coast-to-coast are offered. The company also provides an extensive selection of woven wire-edged ribbons. For information, call the number given above.

Frank's Nursery & Crafts, Inc.
6501 East Nevada
Detroit, MI 48234
313-366-8400

This nationwide company offers a complete and comprehensive selection of quality ribbons, floral supplies, decorative novelties, craft paints, craft sponges, and party supplies. For information, call the number given above or contact the store nearest you.

The Gifted Line, John Grossman, Inc.
999 Canal Blvd.
Point Richmond, CA 94804
1-800-5-GIFTED

For a complete line of gifted boxes, totes, gift wraps, stickers, tags, and cards derived from the John Grossman Collection of Antique Images, call for a store in your area. Products are available in gift and stationery stores nationwide.

Current®
The Current Building
Colorado Springs, CO 80941
1-800-525-7170

This nationwide mail-order company offers a full line of gift wraps and accessories. Roll wraps, assorted sizes of gift bags, coordinated tissues, ribbons, and gift trims are available. Quantity discounts are easily earned.

Harry N. Abrams, Inc.
Attention: Special Sales Department
Department 10
100 Fifth Avenue
New York, NY 10011
212-206-7715, Ext. 506

Gift Wraps By Artists: Drawing upon great
traditions in graphic design and the work of great
individual artists, these wrapping paper books
reproduce classic patterns. Each book features 16
sheets of wrapping paper. For more information,
check with your local bookseller or call the
number given above.

Melissa Neufeld, Incorporated
7060 Koll Center Parkway, Suite 308
Pleasanton, CA 94566
1-800-638-3353

A wide assortment of high-quality papers, stickers,
cards, envelopes, bags, and boxes are offered.
Papers are reproduced from cottage floral designs
and collectibles.

Paper Source, Inc.
232 W. Chicago Ave.
Chicago, IL 60610
312-337-0798

This store offers handmade and exotic papers and
stationery. A wide variety of decorative papers and
commercial grades as well as rubber stamps and
stamping supplies are available.

The Ribbon Outlet, Inc.
3434 Route 22 West, Suite 110
Somerville, NJ 08876
1-800-766-BOWS

For more information on over 3,000 varieties of
first-quality ribbons and trims at factory-direct
savings, call the number given above.

BEAUTIFUL BIRTHDAY

Materials

- 6- × 6- × 4 1/2-inch gift box
- Floral-scented paper drawer liner, cut into a 23- × 12 1/2-inch sheet
- Double-sided tape
- 2 yards of 2 1/4-inch wide lavender, blue, pink, or peach silk moire ribbon, divided into two 1-yard lengths
- Fresh pink, peach, or violet flowers and/or peach silk lilac blossom sprigs

Instructions

1. Using the drawer liner and double-sided tape, wrap the box according to Basic Wrap Directions on page 7. Place the box right-side up. Put a 1-yard ribbon length under the box with equal lengths extending. Bring the ends together at the center. Tie them into a knot. Tie the remaining ribbon length into a bow over the knot.

2. To finish, gently slip the silk or fresh flower stems through the knot of the bow.

Wrapping Options

FOR THE COOK!
For fresh from the oven appeal, trade the scented wrap for a clean white or yellow wrap and top off the sparkling paper with several sticks of cinnamon and a fresh-baked gingerbread cookie.

A MASCULINE TOUCH.
Substitute glossy white or black wrapping paper for the scented paper drawer liner. A brown or red ribbon, a pinecone or sprig of dried flowers, and a gentle spritz of your favorite men's cologne add enough character to suit any deserving male friend.

YESTERYEAR CHARM

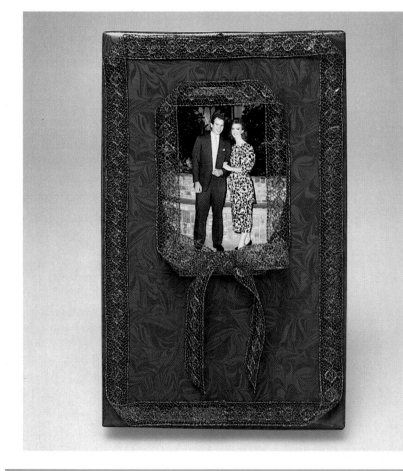

Materials

- 15- × 9 1/2- × 2-inch gift box
- Medium-weight dark green or brown textured wrapping paper, cut into a 25- × 19-inch sheet
- Double-sided tape
- 2 1/2 yards of 1-inch wide gold lace ribbon, divided into 47-, 23-, and 20-inch lengths
- 5- × 7-inch photograph
- All-purpose craft glue

Instructions

1. Using the dark green paper and double-sided tape, wrap the box according to Basic Wrap Directions on page 7. Place the wrapped package right-side up. Using double-sided tape, attach the 47-inch length of ribbon along the outer edges of the package, turning the corners with a diagonal fold.

2. Attach the photograph to the center of the package using double-sided tape. Also attach the 23-inch length of ribbon along the outer edges of the photograph, turning corners with a diagonal fold. Using the remaining 20-inch length of ribbon, tie a bow. Attach it under the photo with the craft glue. Allow to dry.

Wrapping Options

HERE COMES THE BRIDE!
White paper, white lace ribbon, and a cuddly photo of the happy couple is all it takes to turn this nostalgic package into a memory-maker for the future.

BON VOYAGE . . .
The days before the big vacation will tick by extra fast with a cheery reminder. Attach a photo of the destination to the front of the package and border it with a sunny ribbon.

BREAK THE BANK

Materials

- Oversized, sturdy business envelope ($11 \times 4^5/_8$ inches) with velcro or string closure

- Paper money, approximately $5^3/_4 \times 2^3/_4$ inches large

- All-purpose craft glue

- 1 yard of $2^3/_4$-inch wide black silk moire ribbon

Instructions

1. Working from the front to the back of the envelope, attach the paper money using craft glue. Overlap and fold as desired until the envelope is completely covered. Allow to dry.

2. To make the ribbon, place the envelope right-side up. Place the ribbon under the center of the envelope with equal lengths extending from the top and bottom. Bring the ends together at the center. Tie the ends into a bow. Trim as desired.

Wrapping Options

SHORT ON TIME?
Substitute a small box and wrap only the box top with paper money.

SHORT ON PAPER CASH AND TIME?
Rely on a plain white or gray envelope and the same black ribbon. Fold a crisp dollar bill lengthwise and push it through the knot of the bow.

EARLY BIRD SPECIAL

Materials

- 4- × 4- × 4-inch gift box
- Marbled or textured green medium-weight paper, cut into an 18- × 10-inch sheet
- Double-sided tape
- 1¼ yards of ⅛-inch wide yellow paper ribbon or cord
- All-purpose craft glue or hot glue gun
- One 2-inch artificial speckled, white, or yellow bird
- One 2-inch twig bird's nest
- One ½-inch plastic bird egg

Instructions

1. Using the wrapping paper and double-sided tape, wrap the box according to Basic Wrap Directions on page 7. Turn the package upside down. Place the ribbon under the left side of the box with the bottom length extending approximately 4 inches longer than the top left. Bring the ends together at the top-left corner and cross, pulling them tightly in opposite directions. Bring the ribbon ends toward the front of the package, holding them securely in place. Turn the package over. Tie the ends into a small bow. Trim them as desired.

2. For decoration, attach the bird, bird's nest, and egg to the top of the package using craft glue or a hot glue gun. Allow to dry.

HEARTS BELONG TO DADDY

Materials

- Round paper, cardboard, or wood box, approximately 4 to 6 inches in diameter
- 1²/₃ yards of paisley cotton craft ribbon, cut into three 9-inch lengths and two 15-inch lengths
- Hot glue gun or all-purpose craft glue suitable for fabric
- One 3- to 4-inch square or heart-shaped twig wreath
- 8 teal silk or satin rosebuds

Wrapping Option

MOM'S SPECIAL DAY. Mom would enjoy a tasteful box covered with pretty floral ribbons and matching fresh rosebuds. The rosebuds will dry right on the box for a lasting memory of a beautiful day. If you like, glue old buttons to the centers of tiny satiny bows.

1. Working with one of the 15-inch lengths, attach the ribbon to the bottom of the box, gluing the ends to the inside of the bottom. Repeat with the remaining 15-inch ribbon length, making sure that the ribbons cross in the center of the bottom to form an *X*. Allow to dry. Repeat on the box top, using two of the 9-inch lengths.

2. Center the twig wreath on top of the lid using the hot glue gun or craft glue. Attach the silk rosebuds to the wreath using their wire ends.

3. To make the bow, use the remaining 9-inch ribbon length. Form two loops, holding the ribbon securely in the center with thumb and forefinger. Place a small amount of hot glue or craft glue on the back side of the loops. Pinch their center to form a bow. Attach to the top of the box using additional hot glue or craft glue. Allow to dry.

BEAUTY IN THE CHOOSING

Materials

- Floral hand towel or scarf rolled into a 10¹/₂- × 4¹/₂-inch cylinder

- 1 sheet of light purple, pink, yellow, or blue Japanese Kozo tissue paper, pastel unryu tissue paper, or pastel tissue paper, cut into a 21- × 15¹/₂-inch sheet

- Double-sided tape

- 1¹/₃ yards of sheer floral ribbon, cut into two 24-inch lengths

Wrapping Option

FOR ATHLETES ONLY! Showcase a bold swimsuit or striped T-shirt underneath sky blue or cheery red Japanese Kozo tissue paper. A vivid red or blue striped ribbon accentuates the fun bundle inside.

Instructions

1. Place the sheet of tissue paper wrong-side up with the long side facing front. Center the gift on the bottom half of the paper. Pull up the bottom half of the paper.

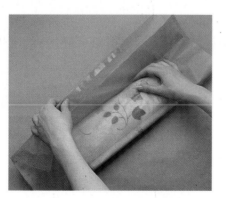

2. Fold the top end of the paper down two inches and fold over the gift. Use double-sided tape to secure.

3. Turn the package right-side up. Working with one end at a time, gather the tissue together at the ends of the package. Tie each end with one of the 24-inch lengths of ribbon forming a bow. Trim the ribbon ends as desired.

THE BIG DAY

Materials

- 15- × 9¹/₂- × 2-inch gift box
- 1 oversized black-and-white calendar page, approximately 25 × 19 inches
- Double-sided tape
- 2 yards of 2¹/₄-inch wide, red or black paper ribbon or grosgrain ribbon
- Black construction paper or felt
- All-purpose craft glue

Wrapping Option

A HOMEMADE CALENDAR. It's easy to create your own calendar page. First, cut white craft paper into a 24- × 18-inch sheet. Next, create a calendar grid for the appropriate month using a ruler and felt-tip markers.

Instructions

1. Using the calendar page and double-sided tape, wrap the box according to Basic Wrap Directions on page 7, making sure that the date for the big day is on the front of the package.

2. To make the ribbon, place the wrapped package right-side up. Place the ribbon over the bottom-left corner of the box with equal ends extending. Pass the ends under and over the bottom-right and top-left corners. Bring the ends together at the top-right corner and tie tightly into a single knot.

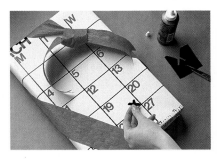

3. For decoration, cut a 1-inch *X* using black construction paper or felt. Attach the *X* on the bottom right of the appropriate square for the big day.

IN THE BLACK

Materials

- $11^1/2$- × $8^1/2$- × $1^1/2$- inch gift box
- 1 newspaper page from the financial section
- Double-sided tape
- 2 yards of black-and-white striped ribbon, black ribbon, or white ribbon, divided into 45- and 27-inch lengths
- Black felt-tip pen
- Alphabet stencil

Wrapping Option

LIGHTEN UP!
If the financial pages are too serious for your carefree friend, offer a colorful package cleverly wrapped in the comic pages of the newspaper.

Instructions

1. Using the newspaper page and double-sided tape, wrap the box according to Basic Wrap Directions found on page 7. Place the longer ribbon over the bottom-right corner of the box with equal lengths extending. Pass the ends under and over the bottom-left and top-right corners. Bring the ends together at the top-left corner and tie them in a knot.

2. Tie the remaining 27 inches of ribbon in a loose single knot over the first knot. Trim the ends to 4 inches or the desired length.

3. Use the stencil and your favorite black felt-tip marker to form the name of the gift-getter. (An alternative to a stencil is a rubber stamp kit. Just stamp the name of the gift-getter on the box.)

SOUTHWESTERN SKIES

Materials

- 4- × 4- × 4-inch gift box
- Textured handmade paper (or art paper) in tan, beige, or harvest gold, cut into an 18- × 10-inch sheet
- Double-sided tape
- Acrylic paints in Southwestern hues
- Small shallow dishes or disposable containers
- Decorative 1- × 3-inch Southwestern motif craft sponges
- 2 strands of red (or natural) raffia or mailing string, each approximately 48 inches long
- 22 inches of 1³/₈-inch wide Southwestern-style ribbon (or red, teal, or gold ribbon) divided into 14- and 8-inch lengths
- Decorative red chili pepper or other Southwestern decoration

Instructions

1. Cover the work surface with a layer of cardboard or plastic. Place the handmade paper on top of the cardboard. Using double-sided tape, wrap the box according to Basic Wrap Directions on page 7. Place a small amount (about the size of a quarter) of each acrylic paint in individual shallow dishes or disposable containers. Thin each paint with water until the mixture is the consistency of heavy cream. Working with one sponge at a time, dip the sponge into the paint until saturated, but not dripping. Blot once onto paper towel to remove excess color. Gently stamp the sponge on the side of the box in the desired position. Thoroughly rinse the sponge in warm water. Repeat with the remaining sponges until box sides are randomly covered as desired. Allow to dry.

2. Center the raffia strands underneath the box. Tie them in a tight knot on top of the box. Trim as desired. Using the 14-inch length of the Southwestern-style ribbon, form a single loop, holding the ends together in the center. Tie the 8-inch length of ribbon in a knot over the loop.

3. Trim the ends of the raffia strands to 1 inch, reserving one of the trimmed lengths. Tie the bow and chili pepper through the center knot to the center of the package with reserved trimming.

AND THE WINNER IS

Materials

- Rose, beige, mauve, or tan handmade paper, torn or cut into an 18- × 12-inch sheet
- All-purpose craft glue
- 32 inches of gold decorative wire
- Artificial leaf and pinecone sprig or fresh rosemary sprig
- Dried pepper berry or bittersweet sprig

Wrapping Option

FOR THE KIDDIES!
Boldly colored construction paper and an attention-grabbing cartoon sticker are all you'll need to make a kid-pleasing envelope.

Instructions

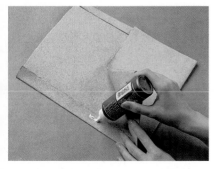

1. To make the envelope, fold the long sides of the paper in 1 inch, pressing firmly to create a sharp crease. Secure each fold with glue. Fold the bottom up 6 inches. Secure the sides with glue. Allow to dry.

2. Fold down the top 4 inches, overlapping the previously folded portion to create an envelope. Press the fold firmly to create a sharp crease.

3. For decoration, place the wire under the envelope with equal lengths extending from top to bottom. Bring the ends together at the center. Tie the ribbon into a bow, catching the pinecone bough and pepper berry sprig in the knot of the bow. Firmly press the knot of the bow to secure the decorations.

IT'S A DAD'S WORLD

Materials

- 11- × 2¹/₂- × 1¹/₄-inch gift box
- ³/₄ yard of plaid or flannel fabric, cut into 15¹/₂- × 6¹/₂-inch and 13¹/₂- × 5¹/₂-inch pieces
- All-purpose craft glue suitable for fabric
- ³/₄ yard of black cord or string
- Decorative plastic gemstone
- Aluminum foil
- 3 Western shirt buttons

Wrapping Option

MOM NEEDS A BREAK, TOO.
For a feminine yet equally Western touch, choose calico fabric, lacy buttons, and a velvety cord.

Instructions

1. Place the 15¹/₂- × 6-inch piece of fabric on work surface, wrongside up. Center the bottom of the box on top of the fabric. Wrap the bottom according to Basic Wrap Directions on page 7, using craft glue to secure the fabric to the inside of the bottom. Allow to dry. Repeat using the 13¹/₂- × 5¹/₂- inch piece of fabric and the top of the box. Allow to dry.

2. Place the box face down. Put the black cord under the box with equal lengths extending. Bring the ends together at the center and cross them, pulling tightly. Bring the ends toward the front of the package. Turn the package over. Repeat the steps. Pass the ends toward the top of the package under the first cord. Tie the ends into a single knot.

3. Separate the cords, pushing them toward the top and bottom to form a modified bow tie. Attach the decorative gemstone in the center of the cords using glue. To decorate the ends of the cords, wrap small pieces of aluminum foil around them. Using glue, attach the buttons, forming a vertical row beneath the tie.

MOM'S SPECIAL DAY

Materials

- Oval or round hat box, $11 \times 8 \times 5\frac{1}{2}$ inches
- Plastic foam flower arranger
- Hot glue gun or all-purpose craft glue
- 5 to 7 large paper or silk flowers
- 2 yards of $1\frac{5}{8}$- inch wide deep violet or burnt orange wire-edged silk or nylon ribbon

Wrapping Option

GO HAT BOX CRAZY.
Having trouble finding the perfect hat box? It's easy to create one of your own. Cover a Shaker-style wooden or cardboard box available in craft stores with craft glue and the paper that's just right for your mom.

Instructions

1. Center the flower arranger on the lid of the hat box. Glue on with the hot glue gun or craft glue. Allow to dry.

2. Trim the paper or silk flower stems to 4 inches. Press the stems into the plastic foam flower arranger as desired.

3. Place the ribbon around the rim of the lid with equal lengths extending. Bring the ends together at the center and tie them into a bow. Using a small amount of hot glue or craft glue, secure the ribbon to the back and sides of the lid. Allow to dry.

BLACK TIE BOTTLE

Instructions

1. Place the black wrapping paper wrong-side up on work surface with the short side facing front. In the center, draw a $3^{1}/_{2}$- inch vertical line $9^{1}/_{2}$ inches from the bottom of the paper. At the top of the $3^{1}/_{2}$- inch line, draw a 1-inch perpendicular line forming a T. Lightly draw two diagonal lines connecting the sides of the T. Slit the vertical and horizontal lines with a craft knife or sharp scissors. Layer the white paper, wrong-side up, over the black paper.

3. To wrap the top of the package, pleat the sides. Fold the top down $^{1}/_{2}$ inch. Secure with tape. Fold down 1 more inch. Secure with tape.

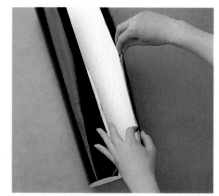

2. Place the bottle onto the layered paper 1 inch from the bottom, centering the bottle over the slit. Hold the bottle securely in place with one hand, folding one side of the paper toward the center of the bottle. Secure with tape. Finish wrapping the bottle according to Basic Wrap Directions on page 7.

4. For decoration, gently fold back the black paper to the diagonal line, forming lapels. Press lightly to crease. To make the cummerbund, place the $10^{1}/_{2}$- inch length of ribbon over the front of the package at the base of the slit. Bring the ribbon ends toward the back of the package. Secure with tape. Trace the bow tie, button, and glove patterns from page 62 onto tracing paper. Cut them out. Trace the bow tie and buttons onto additional black wrapping paper and the gloves onto additional white wrapping paper. Cut them out. Attach them to the front of the package using craft glue.

Materials

- Gift bottle
- Black glossy medium-weight wrapping paper, cut into a $16^{1}/_{2}$- × 13-inch sheet, depending on bottle size
- Quilted white paper, cut into a $16^{1}/_{2}$- × 13-inch sheet, depending on bottle size
- Ruler
- Craft knife or sharp scissors
- $10^{1}/_{2}$ inches of black-and-silver ribbon or desired shimmery plaid ribbon
- Double-sided tape
- All-purpose craft glue
- Bow tie, button, and glove pattern (see page 62)

Wrapping Options

A MATTER OF TIME.
When you want your bottled gift to look formal and you don't have much time, choose a black bottle bag available at party stores. Gather the bag at the top to form a bundle and decorate it as shown.

CASUAL BY CHOICE.
For a quiet weekend dinner with close friends, a less formal wrap is fitting. To achieve an easy-going wrap, substitute a bright green or blue wrapping paper for the black. For the underwrap, replace the white with a fun stripe or cheery print. And trade the cummerbund for a casual ribbon or cord in a contrasting bright color.

SUGARPLUM FANTASY

Instructions

1. Working with one piece of fruit at a time, place a small amount of hot glue (about the size of a quarter) on one side of the fruit. Press the fruit to the basket, about ½ inch below the rim. Hold the fruit in place until the glue is partially dry. Add additional glue if necessary. Repeat with remaining fruit and glue, attaching them approximately 2½ inches apart.

2. Working with 2-inch pieces of green floral wire, attach ivy sprigs to the inside rim of the basket. Make sure that ivy sprigs fill in between fruits and slightly overhang the basket rim.

Materials

- Oval or rectangular gift basket (12 × 8 inches or less)
- Approximately 14 pieces of assorted artificial or papier-mâché fruits (pears, apples, plums, oranges, lemons, etc.) approximately 4 × 3 inches or 2 × 2½ inches large
- Hot glue gun
- Fresh or artificial ivy sprigs or greenery
- Green floral wire, cut into 2-inch lengths
- 3½ yards of 2-inch wide silk lavender and burgundy ribbons, divided into two 45- and two 18-inch lengths
- Food gift
- Iridescent or clear cellophane wrap, cut into a 52- × 36-inch sheet

3. Using the two 45-inch ribbon lengths, tie a single knot around the base of the front basket handle. Weave the ends of the ribbon between the fruit pieces and ivy, meeting the ribbon ends in the back of the basket. If necessary, use a small amount of hot glue to secure the ribbon to the basket rim.

4. Put the food gift in the basket. Center the basket on top of the cellophane wrap. Make sure the handle is parallel to the length of the cellophane paper. Lift up the long ends of the paper, gathering them up to form a bundle. Tie the remaining two 18-inch ribbon lengths in a single knot around the gathered cellophane.

Wrapping Option

DAYS OF WINE AND ROSES!
The perfect way to enjoy a breezy summer evening is to wire fresh and colorful roses and fresh leaves to the rim of the basket and to fill the basket with the wine of your choice.

REGAL VINTAGE

Instructions

1. Enlarge the pattern on page 64 using the dimensions provided onto lightweight cardboard or tracing paper. Using both taffeta pieces, cut two patterns for each color. Working with the two blue pieces, match the right sides together. Using a ¹/₂-inch seam allowance and thread to match the fabric, sew the sides and bottom of the bag together. Repeat using the burgundy pieces. Turn the bags right-side out.

2. Press the seams. Match the side seams at the top of the bag. Using a ¹/₂-inch seam allowance and midnight blue thread, sew around the tops of bags, leaving a 3-inch gap for turning the burgundy bag. Turn the burgundy bag right-side out. You should end up with the burgundy bag on one side and the midnight blue bag on the other.

Materials

- One 15- × 9-inch rectangular bag pattern (see page 64)
- ¹/₃ yard of midnight blue silk taffeta or desired jewel tone
- Midnight blue thread
- ¹/₃ yard of burgundy silk taffeta or desired jewel tone
- Burgundy thread
- Gift bottle
- 1¹/₄ yards of 2-inch wide copper wire-edged nylon ribbon
- Straight pins

3. Push the burgundy bag inside of the blue bag. Whipstitch the opening to close.

4. For giving, place the desired wine in the bag. Tie the ribbon into a bow around the top of the filled bag. Crimp the wire ribbon ends as desired.

Wrapping Options

ELEGANT EFFECTS WITHOUT SEWING!
If you're short on sewing time, you can achieve the same stunning looks with a deep blue or violet bottle bag available in card and party stores. Adorn with a satiny peach, copper, or burgundy bow, and you're set.

ANOTHER OPTION!
Check out your scrap fabric pile. Select a richly colored floral or plaid. Cut the fabric into a square approximately 22 × 22 inches. Place the desired bottle in the center and bundle the fabric around the bottle. A contrasting ribbon completes the look.

GROOMED IN VELVET

Instructions

1. Place the 31- × 31-inch piece of velvet on work surface, wrong-side up. Drizzle a line of glue around the outer edges of the box bottom. Center the bottom on top of the velvet. Wrap the bottom according to Basic Wrap Directions on page 7, using the craft glue to secure the velvet to the inside of the box. Trim extra fabric as needed when executing folds. Allow to dry. Repeat using the 15- × 15-inch piece of velvet and the top of the box. Allow to dry.

2. Place the velvet box right-side up. Put the floral arranger on the top-left corner of the box. Glue it on using the craft glue. To make the ribbon, place the 2-yard piece of ribbon over the bottom-right corner of the box with equal lengths extending. Pass the ends under and over the bottom-left and top-right corners. Bring the ends together at the top-left corner over the flower arranger. Tie them tightly into a single knot over the flower arranger to secure.

3. For decoration, press the ends of the silk flowers and grapes into the flower arranger. Trim the ribbon ends as desired.

4. Pass one of the 1¹/₄- yard ribbon lengths under the first knot. Bring the ends together. Tie into a bow over the first knot. Repeat using the remaining ribbon length.

Materials

- 10 - × 10 - × 9-inch rigid gift box with separate top and bottom
- 1 yard of 60-inch wide midnight blue velvet, cut into a 31- × 31-inch piece and a 15- × 15-inch piece
- All-purpose craft glue suitable for fabric
- One 3- to 4-inch plastic foam flower arranger
- 4¹/₂ yards of 2-inch wide gold wire-edged nylon ribbon, cut into one 2-yard length and two 1¹/₄-yard lengths
- Assorted dusty rose and blue silk flowers
- 2 small bunches of artificial blue or dusty rose grapes

Wrapping Options

JEWELED IN VELVET. Nothing makes a special gift of jewelry sparkle more than a keepsake velvet box. Wrap a petite box in a soft pink, green, or beige velvet and tie it with a pretty silk or taffeta ribbon.

TIME TO PULL OUT ALL THE STOPS. Top off a feminine velvety pink wrap with a fresh, deep red rose bouquet. The roses will dry right on the box for an everlasting keepsake.

THE HAPPY TWOSOME

Instructions

1. Using the wrapping paper and double-sided tape, wrap the box according to Basic Wrap Directions on page 7. Center the photograph on top of the wrapped package using double-sided tape. With the wrong side of each facing up, layer the white, blue, yellow, and pink pearlized tissue paper. Staple the corners of the sheets together to avoid slipping. Place the package in the center of the layered tissue paper. Using a pencil, lightly trace around the outer edges of the package on the paper.

2. Draw a 4-inch diameter circle in the center of the traced paper. Sketch perpendicular lines in the center of the circle. Using a craft knife or sharp scissors, cut slits over the perpendicular lines, forming four triangles.

3. Place two strips of double-sided tape on each end of the package. Place package, wrong-side up, over the traced tissue paper. Wrap according to Basic Wrap Directions. To frame the photo, gently roll each triangle of layered tissue paper away from the center of the photo with a pencil. Secure each roll with a small piece of tape.

4. To make the bow, place the ribbon over the bottom-right corner of the box with equal lengths extending. Pass the ends under and over the bottom-left and top-right corners. Bring the ends together at the top-left corner and tie loosely into a single knot. Trim the ends to approximately 2$\frac{1}{2}$ inches or to desired length.

Materials

- 9- × 4$\frac{1}{2}$- × 4$\frac{1}{2}$- inch gift box
- Silver matte-finished medium-weight wrapping paper, cut into a 20- × 15$\frac{1}{2}$-inch sheet
- Double-sided tape
- 5- × 7-inch horizontal photograph of the engaged couple receiving the gift
- Two 30- × 20-inch sheets each: white, blue, yellow, and pink pearlized tissue paper
- Craft knife or sharp scissors
- 1$\frac{1}{3}$ yards of 1$\frac{1}{4}$- inch wide floral, pink, blue, or yellow paper ribbon

Wrapping Options

MISSING A PHOTO?
You can still wrap an extra-special package. Trade the photo for your own special insert. How about two hearts with the couple's names expertly inscribed or better yet—the date of their engagement.

SPORTY TAILORING.
Everyone has a favorite sport, whether it's baseball, golf, or ping pong! The appropriate insert—be it a baseball card or a photo of walking accessories—will show the recipient you care.

FROM THIS DAY FORWARD

Instructions

1. Using the wrapping paper and double-sided tape, wrap each box according to Basic Wrap Directions on page 7. Place both boxes right-side up. Cross two pieces of tape in the center of the large box. Stack the smaller box on top of the larger box. Place one 1⅓- yard length of nylon netting under the larger box with equal lengths extending. Bring the ends together at the center and tie a single knot. Repeat with the remaining 1⅓- yard length opposite the first length of netting. Trim one set of ends.

2. Using the 1-yard lengths of netting, tie four freestanding bows. Place two of the bows together to make a double bow, securing them with one of the 12-inch lengths of netting.

Wrapping Option

THE BRIDAL BOUQUET. Let the flower garden do the work. Replace the bows on top of this package with a generous hand-tied bouquet of flowers of your choice. Use a white satin ribbon to secure them on top of the package.

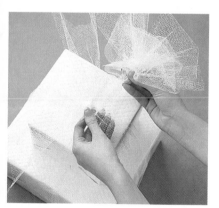

3. Working with the ends of the 12-inch length, tie a double bow on top of the package. Repeat with the remaining bows and 12-inch length of netting, forming a cluster of bows.

4. To make the floral bouquet, insert the ends of the first knot through the bottom of the floral guard. Pull the ends up through the center.

5. Trim the rose stems to 3 inches. Press the stems into the center of the guard.

TA DA TADA; TA DA TADUM

Materials

- 3 1/2- × 3 1/2- × 2-inch gift box

- 1 3/4 yards of 1-inch wide ivory satin ribbon, cut into four 6 1/4- inch lengths and four (or five) 9-inch lengths

- 2 yards of 1-inch wide mauve satin ribbon, cut into four 6 1/4- inch lengths and five (or four) 9-inch lengths

- All-purpose craft glue suitable for fabric

- Small bouquet of miniature artificial flowers

Instructions

1. Attach the four 9-inch ribbon lengths to the box, securing with glue. Allow to dry. Weave the remaining mauve ribbon lengths over and under the white ribbon lengths to create a checkerboard pattern. Allow to dry.

2. Using the remaining 9-inch mauve or ivory ribbon length, tie a bow around the bouquet. Attach the bow to the box using craft glue. Allow to dry.

Wrapping Options

FOR THE GROOM.
Regal colors best reflect the groom's style. Instead of subtle ivory and mauve, weave richly colored forest green and bronze or burgundy satin ribbons. Trade the bouquet for a decorative gold medallion available at fabric stores.

FOR THE BABY.
Weave baby-pleasing grosgrain ribbons to match the happy colors of the little one's nursery.

THE HOLLY AND THE IVY

Materials

- 7- × 7- × 7-inch gift box
- Copper moire medium-weight wrapping paper, cut into a 30- × 16-inch sheet
- Double-sided tape
- 1³/₄- inch plastic foam flower arranger
- All-purpose craft glue
- 3 yards of 1¹/₂- inch wide teal wired silk ribbon, moire ribbon, or satin ribbon, divided into 2¹/₃-yard and ²/₃-yard lengths
- Silk variegated ivy sprigs or fresh variegated ivy sprigs
- Artificial red berry and pinecone boughs or individual holly boughs and small pinecones

Instructions

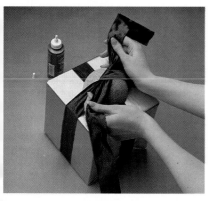

1. Using the wrapping paper and double-sided tape, wrap the box according to Basic Wrap Directions on page 7. Turn the package upside down. Place the 2¹/₃- yard ribbon length under the box with equal lengths extending. Bring the ends together at the center and cross them, pulling them tightly in opposite directions. Bring the ends toward the front of the package, holding them securely in place. Turn the package over. Center the flower arranger on top of the package using craft glue. Allow to dry. Tie the ends into a bow, securing the flower arranger. Crinkle ribbon ends as desired.

2. Press the ends of the ivy, red berries, and pinecones into the plastic foam arranger as desired.

3. Tie the remaining ²/₃- yard of ribbon into a loose single knot over the first knot. Trim the ends as desired.

OH, CHRISTMAS TREE

Materials

- Flat-topped 1½- quart glass jar or acrylic container
- Food gift
- Hot glue gun or all-purpose craft glue
- One 6- to 8-inch miniature artificial Christmas tree
- 2 to 3 miniature holiday gifts
- Miniature tree decorations (star, lights, ornaments, garlands, etc.)
- Green floral wire
- 1 yard of 2 ½-inch wide Christmas ribbon

Wrapping Option

GIFT OF ANOTHER KIND. Top off any small- or medium-sized box with your originally decorated Christmas tree.

Instructions

1. Fill the jar with the food gift as desired. Close or seal the jar. Center the tree on top of the lid with the hot glue gun or craft glue. Allow to dry.

2. Glue the packages under the tree as desired. Allow to dry. Decorate the tree as desired, attaching ornaments with floral wire.

3. To make the bow, circle the ribbon around the lid. Tie the ends into a loose knot. Trim the ends as desired.

SILVER AND GOLD

Materials

- 6- × 6- × 4½- inch gift box
- Cream 90-pound water-color paper, or 80-pound text paper, cut into a 23- × 12½-inch sheet
- Silver acrylic paint
- Gold acrylic paint
- 2 paint brushes, approximately 1¼ inches wide
- Double-sided tape
- 2 yards of 1½- inch wide wire-edged silver nylon ribbon or desired silver ribbon, cut into two 1-yard lengths
- 2 yards of 1½- inch wide wire-edged gold nylon ribbon or desired gold ribbon, cut into two 1- yard lengths
- 1 gold or silver pinecone or silver or gold ball ornament
- Green floral wire

Instructions

1. Cover the work surface with a layer of cardboard or plastic. Put the wrapping paper, right-side up, on cardboard. Place a small amount (about the size of a quarter) of silver paint in a disposable container made of foil or plastic. Thin with water until the mixture is of the consistency of heavy cream. Repeat with the gold paint. Dip the brush into the paint. Starting at the upper corner of the paper, paint silver daubs every two inches using quick brush strokes. Using the gold paint, fill in between the silver strokes. Repeat the rows, alternating the starting color, until the paper is completely covered. Allow to dry.

2. Turn paper wrong-side up. Wrap the box according to Basic Wrap Directions on page 7. To make the ribbons, turn the box right-side up. Slightly overlap two silver and gold 1-yard ribbon lengths, placing them under the box with equal lengths extending. Bring the ends together at the center. Tie the ends in a single knot. Pass one end of the gold 1-yard ribbon length under the first knot. Bring the ends together and tie them into a bow over the first knot. Repeat using the remaining silver 1-yard ribbon length.

3. For decoration, place a small piece of floral wire through the ornament loop or around the pinecone. Attach it to the knot in the center of bows.

HOLIDAY MEMORIES GONE BY

Instructions

1. Trim the holiday cards as desired. Using a small amount of glue, attach the cards to the top of the box, overlapping as desired until the lid is completely covered. Allow to dry. (Extra glue may be required when folding cards around corners and sides of the box lid.) Repeat on the bottom of the box. Allow to dry.

2. To make the ribbon, place the covered box right-side up. Using the 1⅓-yard length of ribbon, place the ribbon under the box with equal lengths extending. Bring the ends together at the center. Tie the ends into a single knot. Tie the 1-yard length into a bow over the first knot.

Materials

- Sturdy box with separate top and bottom, approximately 10½ × 10½ × 2 inches
- Assorted Victorian holiday cards
- All-purpose craft glue
- 3 yards of 1⅜-inch wide crimson moire ribbon, cut into 1⅓-yard, 1-yard, and two ⅓-yard lengths
- Craft sealer••

•• Several coats of craft sealer applied to the top and bottom of this box will add to the keeping qualities of this unique gift. Be sure to allow the craft sealer to dry between coats.

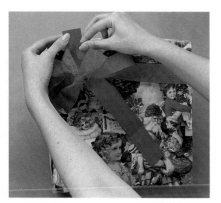

3. To make the double bow, form two loops with one of the ⅓-yard lengths, holding them securely in the center with thumb and forefinger.

4. Using the other ⅓-yard length, tie a bow around the center of the loops. With the ends, tie the second bow to the center of the first bow covering the knot. Trim the ends as desired.

Wrapping Options

SHORT ON CARDS?
First wrap the gift in red, green, or gold moire wrapping paper according to Basic Wrap Directions. Instead of forming a card collage, randomly place a few Victorian or antique cards all over the package.

A HOLIDAY CARD WREATH.
Choose a festive holiday wrap and wrap the box according to Basic Wrap Directions. Cut a few holiday cards into recognizable pieces. Form a wreath on the top of the package using the holiday card pieces.

BE MY VALENTINE

Instructions

1. Using the wrapping paper and double-sided tape, wrap the box according to Basic Wrap Directions on page 7. Place the wrapped package right-side up. Center one doily on each side of the package with a long piece of tape. Make sure that equal portions face front and back.

2. To make the ribbon, carefully turn the package upside down. Place the ribbon under the box with equal lengths extending. Bring the ends together at the center and cross, pulling tightly in opposite directions. Bring the ends toward the front of the package, holding them securely in place. Turn the package over. Tie the ends into a single knot. Trim and shape the ribbon ends as desired.

Materials

- 12- × 8½- × 1-inch gift box

- Pink or red matte-finished wrapping paper, cut into a 21- × 15-inch sheet

- Double-sided tape

- Four 10 × 6½- inch oval white paper doilies

- 2 yards of 1½- inch wide wire-edged pink- or red-striped acetate or silk ribbon or light pink or red satin or acetate satin ribbon

- Eight 9-inch pink or white tulle circles

- White and pink or red candy mints or hearts

- 1⅔ yards of ⅛- inch wide light pink or red satin ribbon or pink or red curling ribbon, cut into four 14-inch lengths

3. For decoration, place eight to ten candies in the center of a double round of pink tulle. Lift all of the sides of the tulle round. Gather the tulle to form a bundle; tie with one of the 14-inch lengths of pink satin ribbon. Repeat with the remaining tulle, candies, and pink satin ribbons.

4. To attach decorations, tie the ends of the pink satin ribbon to the knot in the center of the pink-striped ribbon, forming a cluster of bundles.

Wrapping Options

NO SWEETS FOR YOUR VALENTINE.
A single pink or red rose will decorate this package exceptionally well. Simply tie it to the striped ribbon above using a small piece of satin ribbon.

WHEN ONLY HEARTS WILL DO.
Cut oversized hearts from a contrasting paper and tape them to all sides of the package instead of using oval doilies.

FOR MY BEAU

Materials

- 9- × 4½- × 4½- inch gift box
- White textured handmade paper or white text paper, cut into a 20- × 15½-inch sheet
- Double-sided tape
- Heart-shaped stamp
- Red ink stamp pad
- 1 yard of ⅞- inch wide red satin, silk, or velvet ribbon
- 1 fresh or silk stemmed red flower blossom

Instructions

1. Using the wrapping paper and double-sided tape, wrap the box according to Basic Wrap Directions on page 7. For decoration, press the rubber stamp onto the ink pad; lift; press stamp firmly onto the paper. Repeat until package is covered as desired. Allow to dry.

2. To make the ribbon, place the wrapped package right-side up. Place the ribbon under the box with equal lengths extending. Bring the ends together at the center. Tie the ends into a bow. Slip the stem of the flower through the knot in the bow. Pull the ends of the ribbon tightly to secure the flower.

Wrapping Options

STAMPS AREN'T FOR YOU?
You can rely on easy-to-use heart-shaped stickers. Or better yet, why not create a heart sponge? See page 9 for sponging basics. Another idea is a heart stencil—many craft stores have them in a variety of sizes.

ROSES ARE RED!
Come Valentine's Day, red roses are the flower of choice. For a gift that says it all, simply tie a red rose nosegay to the front of the box.

RIBBONED FOR EASTER

Materials

- White loosely woven basket with handle, approximately 9 to 10 inches in diameter and 5 to 6 inches tall

- Easter gift

- 2 ½ yards each: 1½-inch wide pastel pink, yellow, blue, and green grosgrain ribbon, cut into 22-inch lengths

- Pastel paper straw

- 2 ½ yards each: 6-inch wide pastel pink, yellow, blue, and green tulle or netting

- 2 decorative hand-painted Easter eggs

Instructions

1. Starting at the bottom of the basket and working with one 22-inch ribbon length at a time, weave the ends of the ribbon through a slat in the basket. Bring the ribbon ends together. Tie them into a bow. Repeat with the remaining ribbon lengths until the basket is covered with bows. Alternate bow colors as desired. Fill the basket with straw and add the gift.

2. To enclose the basket, work with one 2 ½-yard length of tulle at a time. Place each tulle length under the basket with equal lengths extending. Bring the ends together at the center, just above the handle. Tie the ends into an oversized bow. Trim the ends as desired. For decoration, loop the Easter egg ornaments around the basket handle.

3. Repeat with the remaining tulle lengths until basket is enclosed. Alternate tulle colors as desired.

AND BABY MAKES THREE

Materials

- White, pink, or blue lace 16-inch round pillowcase
- Baby gift
- Pastel tissue paper
- 2 1/3 yards of 2 1/4-inch wide pastel blue or pink satin ribbon
- 2 1/3 yards of 7/8-inch wide pink and white "baby" ribbon or pink or blue satin ribbon
- Pastel baby rattle
- Pacifier

Wrapping Option

PAPER PILLOW SURPRISE.

For a billowy pillow look without the pillowcase—fashion a sturdy paper pillowcase using a double layer of white, pink, or blue wrapping paper.

Instructions

1. Tuck the gift inside the pillowcase. Add shape with additional tissue paper. Close the pillowcase.

2. To make the ribbon, place the stuffed pillowcase upside down. Put pink ribbon on top of the blue ribbon and place them under the pillow with equal lengths extending. Bring the ends together at the center and cross, pulling gently in opposite directions. Bring the ends toward the front of the pillow. Turn the pillow over. Tie the ends into a single knot.

3. Insert one ribbon end through the rattle. Tie the ribbon ends into a second knot, securing the rattle in place. Trim as desired. For decoration, insert one pink ribbon end through the pacifier. Tie the ends into a single knot.

IT'S A GIRL

Materials

- 10- × 7- × 1½-inch gift box
- White craft paper, cut into a 19- × 13½-inch sheet
- Double-sided tape
- Pink and blue double-sided art pens
- Decorative ribbon and bow stencil
- Four 1- to 2-inch plastic baby decorations
- All-purpose craft glue
- 22 inches of pink grosgrain ribbon

Wrapping Option

IT'S A BOY!
Trade the pink bow for a blue one. Stencil the ribbons and bows with the blue pen instead of the pink one.

Instructions

1. Using the white craft paper and double-sided tape, wrap the box according to Basic Wrap Directions on page 7. Using the pink art pen, draw 3 horizontal lines spaced 1½ inches apart on the front of the box. Hand-letter the birth announcement with the blue art pen.

2. Using the ribbon stencil and pink art pen, stencil the ribbon pattern around the outer edge of the package. Attach the baby decorations using craft glue.

3. Tie the pink grosgrain ribbon into a bow. Place a small amount of glue on the back of the bow. Put the bow in the center of the bottom border. Allow to dry.

25 HEARTS

Materials

- 7- × 7- × 7-inch gift box
- White glossy paper, cut into a 30- × 16-inch sheet
- Double-sided tape
- Twenty-five 3-inch silver doily hearts
- All-purpose craft glue
- 2 $\frac{1}{3}$ yards of 4$\frac{3}{4}$- inch wide white and silver organza drawstring ribbon, cut into 1$\frac{1}{3}$-yard and 1-yard lengths
- Decorative silver *25*

Wrapping Option

50 YEARS INSTEAD.
A golden anniversary is even more special. Instead of the doilies, you can use smaller 1$\frac{1}{2}$- inch gold stickers instead. They're easier and quicker to apply.

Instructions

1. Using the wrapping paper and double-sided tape, wrap the box according to Basic Wrap Directions on page 7. Attach the hearts to the top, bottom, and sides of the package using double-sided tape or craft glue. Remember to add 5 hearts to the bottom of the box in order to use the full 25.

2. Gather the ribbon lengths by pulling gently on the white drawstrings. Place the gathered 1$\frac{1}{3}$-yard ribbon length under the box with equal lengths extending. Bring the ends together at the center and tie the strings into a knot.

3. Pass the end of the 1-yard ribbon length under the knot of the first ribbon. Bring the ends together at the center. Tie them into a bow. Insert the silver *25* through the knot in the bow.

GHOSTS AND GOBLINS

Materials

- One 1-gallon tin canister approximately 8 inches high
- White craft paper, cut into a 26- × 24-inch square
- Pumpkin stencil (see page 62)
- Double-sided tape
- Transparent tape
- Black acrylic paint
- Orange acrylic paint
- 2 shallow dishes or disposable containers
- White artist tape or masking tape
- Porous sponge or medium stencil brush
- 1½ yards of 2¾-inch wide natural or orange mesh ribbon
- 1 yard of 2½-inch wide wire-edged pumpkin ribbon

Instructions

1. Cover the work surface with a layer of cardboard or plastic. Place the craft paper, right-side up, on cardboard. Trace the pumpkin stencil onto a piece of cardboard or plastic. Cut out the stencil. Using a pencil, draw a faint line on the paper 4½ inches from the bottom edge of the paper. Place a small amount (about the size of a quarter) of both paints into disposable foil or plastic containers. Position the stencil on the white paper, making sure the pattern does not go below the traced line. Anchor the stencil with artist tape or masking tape at the corners. Dip the sponge into the paint. Blot gently onto paper towel to remove excess color. Gently press the sponge within the design, using an up-and-down motion to apply the paint. When done, carefully remove the stencil. Repeat using the stencil and paints until the paper is covered as desired. Wipe the stencil each time it is moved to prevent smears. Allow to dry. Gently erase the traced pencil line. Place the paper on the work surface, unpainted side up. Center the canister 4½ inches from the bottom of the paper and wrap it.

2. Gradually fold in the paper at the bottom of the tin, layering each new fold over the last. Secure with tape. Fold in the paper at the top of the tin, again layering each new fold over the last.

3. Gather the folds to form a bundle. Layer 1-yard lengths of mesh and pumpkin ribbons. Tie the ribbons loosely around the bundle. Use scissors to zigzag the top as desired.

49

A TOUCH OF CLASS

Instructions

Materials

- 11½- × 8½- × 1½- inch gift box
- Black glossy medium-weight wrapping paper, cut into a 15- × 22-inch sheet
- Silver acrylic paint
- Paint brush, approximately 1¼ inches wide
- Small shallow dish or disposable container
- Double-sided tape
- 2 yards of 1½-inch wide black-and-silver, black, or silver metallic ribbon
- White craft paper, cut into an 8½- × 6-inch sheet
- 16 inches of silver curling ribbon

1. Cover the work surface with a layer of cardboard or plastic. Place the black wrapping paper right-side up on the cardboard. Place a small amount (about the size of a quarter) of silver paint in a disposable container made of foil or plastic. Thin the paint with water until the mixture is of drizzling consistency. Dip the paint brush into the paint. Gently shake the brush over the paper, drizzling the paint randomly. Repeat until you have covered the paper with paint as desired. Allow to dry.

2. Turn the wrapping paper wrong-side up. Wrap the box according to Basic Wrap Directions on page 7. Turn the package upside down. Place the ribbon under the box with equal lengths extending. Bring the ends together at the center and cross them, pulling tightly in opposite directions. Bring the ends toward the front of the package, holding them securely in place. Turn the package over. Tie the ends with a single knot. Tie them again into a loose double knot. Trim the ends to 6 inches, or whatever length you prefer.

Wrapping Options

SILVER BELLS, SILVER BELLS!
It certainly is Christmas time. Make the holiday season extra special with a luscious silver package. Instead of black paper, use white paper and drizzle it with silver paint as directed above. A silver mesh ribbon and plastic silver bells will make your holiday creation hard to resist.

HERE COMES PETER COTTONTAIL!
Peter Cottontail prefers shades of spring as he hops down the bunny trail. Drizzle white paper as directed above with cheery shades of pink, blue, green, and yellow. A perky polka-dot ribbon and a bundle of jelly beans make hunting for Easter eggs extra special.

3. Roll the white craft paper into a scroll. Tie 16 inches of curling ribbon around the scroll. Curl the ribbon ends. Gently dip the ends of the scroll into the remaining silver paint. Shake off excess. Allow to dry.

4. Tie the painted scroll by slipping the remaining curling ribbon under the knot at the center of the package.

THE FARMER IN THE DELL

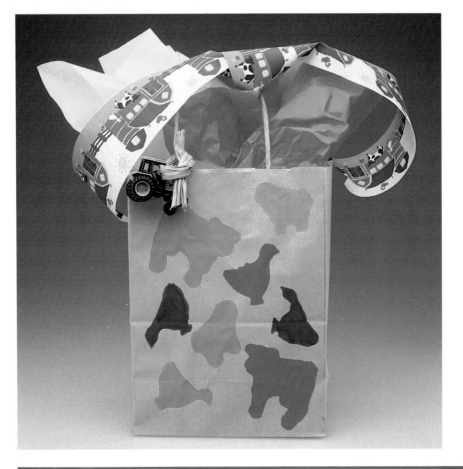

Materials

- Brown paper gift bag (11 × 8 inches or larger)
- Acrylic paints in assorted colors such as red, blue, green, orange, and yellow
- Small shallow dishes or disposable containers
- Decorative 1- to 3-inch farm animal craft sponges
- Red tissue paper
- Yellow tissue paper
- 1 yard of 3-inch wide farm-scene ribbon
- 2- to 3-inch plastic farm toy or farm animal
- Natural paper ribbon

Instructions

1. Cover the work surface with a layer of cardboard or plastic. Place brown bag on work surface. Flatten it. Place a small amount (about the size of a quarter) of each acrylic paint in individual shallow dishes or dispos-

able containers. Thin each paint with water until the mixture is the consistency of heavy cream. Working with one sponge at a time, dip the sponge into the paint until saturated, but not dripping. Blot once onto paper towel to remove excess color. Gently stamp the sponge on the paper bag. Thoroughly rinse the sponge in warm water. Repeat with the remaining sponges until the top side of the bag is randomly covered. Allow to dry. Turn the bag over. Using the same sponges and paints, randomly cover the bag with sponged animals. Allow to dry.

2. When dry, place the gift inside the bag. Line the bag with red and yellow tissue paper. Tie the bag handles together using farm-scene ribbon tied in a single knot. Using the natural paper ribbon, tie the farm toy to the bag handle.

A GIRL'S WORLD

Materials

- $11^{1}/_{2}$- × $8^{1}/_{2}$- × $1^{1}/_{2}$-inch gift box
- Rose blossom wrapping paper, cut into a 22- × 15-inch sheet
- Double-sided tape
- Old-fashioned paper doll and outfits
- 2 yards of $2^{1}/_{2}$-inch wide pink pastel paper ribbon

Instructions

1. Using the wrapping paper and double-sided tape, wrap the box according to Basic Wrap Directions on page 7. Cut out the paper doll and desired outfits. Using a short piece of tape, attach the doll and outfits to the front of the package, overlapping as desired. (Use only enough tape to secure the doll and outfits to the package to allow the recipient to use them later.)

2. Place the box right-side up. Using a 2-yard length of ribbon, place the ribbon under the box with equal ends extending. Bring the ends together at the center. Tie the ends into a bow. Trim as desired.

Wrapping Options

CRAFTED FROM THE HEART.
Instead of using store-bought paper dolls, create whimsical "stick people" using plain white craft paper and scissors. Hand-color your new dolls with crayons, colored markers, or poster paint. If you like, use the crayons to create your own fanciful fashions.

ESPECIALLY FOR THE HOLIDAYS.
Let your seasonal style prevail! Using plain white or brown craft paper and scissors, create eye-catching paper doll garlands in a variety of designs. How about bouncing bunnies for Easter, gingerbread men for Christmas, hearts for Valentines, and pumpkins for Halloween? Attach them in graphic rows to a box wrapped in the solid paper of your choice.

SUMMER FUN

Materials

- 3 to 4 small packages, approximately $7 \times 5 \times 1\frac{1}{2}$ inches and smaller
- Neon tennis shoe wrapping paper or other patterned neon paper
- Double-sided tape
- Red or pink cellophane, cut into two 30- × 30-inch sheets
- 1 set of green or pink neon shoe strings or 2 yards of $\frac{1}{4}$-inch wide neon satin or grosgrain ribbon cut into 1-yard lengths
- Yellow or green neon glasses or desired neon decoration

Instructions

1. Using the wrapping paper and double-sided tape, wrap the small boxes according to Basic Wrap Directions on page 7. Layer the sheets of red cellophane. Stack the small packages, placing the largest package on the bottom. Center the stack of packages on the cellophane. Lift four corners of the cellophane up; gather and tie one of the neon strings into a single knot.

Cross the ends of the neon string in the back of the bundle. Cross again in the front. Tie the string into a bow. Repeat with the remaining neon string, ending with the bow facing back.

2. For decoration, place the neon sunglasses on the front of the bundle by pushing the stem ends between the strands of the neon string.

Wrapping Option

IT'S ALREADY NEON BRIGHT!
Come summertime, everything takes on a neon hue. Forget the boxes and neon wrapping paper. Instead, roll or bundle the bright cellophane around the gift as desired for a super fun effect.

COLORING BOOK BIRTHDAY

Materials

- 9- × 4¹/₂- × 4¹/₂- inch gift box
- 1 oversized coloring book page, approximately 20 × 15¹/₂ inches
- Double-sided tape
- 5 crayons in assorted colors
- All-purpose craft glue or hot glue gun
- 2 yards of primary color ribbon, cut into 1¹/₄- yard, 15-inch, and 12-inch lengths

Instructions

1. Using the coloring book page and double-sided tape, wrap the box according to Basic Wrap Directions on page 7. Place the 1¹/₄- yard of ribbon over the bottom-right corner of the box with equal lengths extending. Pass the ends under and over the bottom-left and top-right corners. Bring the ends together at the top-left corner and tie them tightly into a single knot.

2. Place the 12-inch ribbon length under the crayons with equal lengths extending. Tie them into a single knot. Using the craft glue, attach the crayon bundle. Using a red crayon, hand-color the recipient's name or desired Happy Birthday message. Tie the 15-inch ribbon length into a bow over the first knot.

Wrapping Option

CRAYON BONANZA!
When an oversized coloring book isn't available, you can have fun drawing your own imaginative coloring book wrap. Substitute a sheet of white craft paper and color. If you like, you can skip the ribbons and hand-color your own festive crayon bow.

LEAVING THE NEST

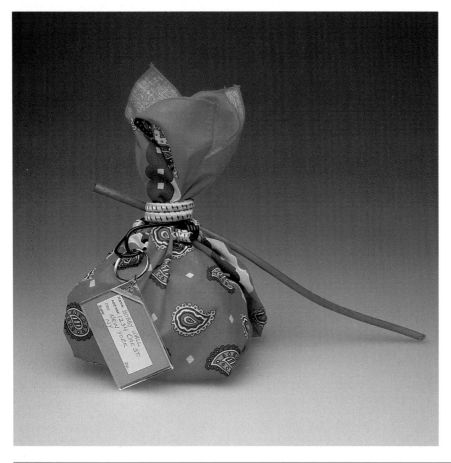

Materials

- 21- × 21-inch bandanna
- White tissue paper
- One 12- to 14-inch elastic cord
- Acrylic luggage tag
- 14-inch stick, dowel, or bamboo

Wrapping Option

OFF TO CAMP.
Even if you don't have a colorful bandanna on hand, you can still send your youngster off to camp in style. Using a crayon or magic marker, write your favorite camper's name all over the outside of a sturdy brown paper bag. Place your gift in the bag and fold the top down 2 inches. Gather the top to form a bundle and tie it with a perky cord or ribbon.

Instructions

1. Place the gift in the center of the bandanna. Pad with scrunched tissue paper to form a bundle. Lift all the corners of the bandanna.

2. Neatly gather the bandanna to form a bundle. Wrap elastic cord around the bundle to secure it, closing it in front.

3. Attach the luggage tag to the elastic cord. Push the end of the stick under the cord.

CAUGHT AT SEA

Materials

- Yellow, red, or blue sand pail, 8 to 10 inches high
- Bright green or blue crepe or tissue paper, cut into a 30- × 30-inch sheet
- 2½ yards of yellow curling ribbon, cut into one 1½-yard and two 18-inch lengths
- 1½ yards each: red, blue, and green curling ribbon
- Red net tote bag
- 1 sand toy, such as a rake, shovel, or scoop

Wrapping Option

FOR THE FISHERMAN'S BIRTHDAY.

All a fisherman requires is a net with which to reel in a big catch. Bundle the gift as below, then place it directly into the net.

Instructions

1. Place the gift in the center of the crepe paper. Pad with additional scrunched crepe paper, if desired. Lift all corners of the crepe paper. Gather the paper to form a bundle. Place the wrapped gift in the sand pail.

2. Add the 1½ yards of yellow curling ribbon to the red, blue, and green curling ribbon. Place the layered ribbons around the top of the bundle with equal lengths extending. Tie them into a single knot and then into a bow, separating the loops to show the different colors. Place the sand pail into the net bag.

3. Lift the handles of the net bag. Insert the toy rake through each handle. Secure the rake by tying the remaining 18-inch yellow ribbon lengths into a single knot around each handle just beneath the toy rake.

A CLOWN ESCAPADE

Materials

- Bright yellow, orange, or purple gift bag, approximately 11 × 8 inches
- Assorted clown stickers
- 8 to 10 small balloons in bright colors such as orange, red, blue, green, and purple
- Hot glue gun or all-purpose craft glue
- Tissue paper in blue, green, and purple
- Paper curling ribbon in green, purple, and pink

Wrapping Option

BALLOONS FOR ADULTS?
You bet! Consider a black or silver bag with white balloons, stickers, and curling ribbons as a winning combination.

Instructions

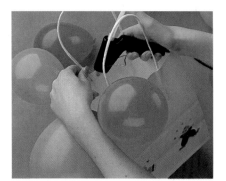

1. Working with a flattened bag, attach the stickers to the front, back, and sides of the bag until it is covered as desired.

2. Blow up the balloons as recommended on the package. Using the hot glue gun or craft glue, place a small amount of glue inside the bag approximately one-half inch from the top. Gently press the end of the balloons against the glue to secure. Repeat until all balloons are attached to the bag.

3. Fill the bag with tissue paper as desired. Loop the paper curling ribbon around the handles.

58

ROCKETS IN SPACE

Materials

- 12-inch mailing cylinder, approximately 4 inches in diameter
- Red glossy wrapping paper, cut into a 14- × 12-inch sheet
- Double-sided tape
- Rocket booster pattern (see page 63)
- Tracing paper
- Yellow foam board
- Craft knife or sharp scissors
- Hot glue gun or all-purpose craft glue
- Star or polka-dot party hat
- Transparent tape
- Silver star or circle name tag

Instructions

1. Using the red wrapping paper and double-sided tape, wrap the cylinder according to Basic Wrap Directions on page 7. Trace the pattern onto lightweight tracing paper. Cut it out. Trace the pattern twice on the foam board. Turn the booster over. Trace the pattern two more times. (You will have 4 boosters.) Using a craft

knife or sharp scissors, cut out all 4 of the traced rocket boosters. Match the rocket boosters, making sure the yellow sides face front and back. Glue them together. Allow to dry.

2. Glue the rocket boosters to the sides of the cylinder.

3. Attach the party hat to the cylinder. Secure the elastic strap to the bottom of the cylinder using transparent tape. Place the name tag over the party hat, securing with tape if desired.

SPRINGTIME MAGIC

Instructions

1. Enlarge the pattern found on page 63 using the dimensions provided onto lightweight cardboard or tracing paper. Cut it out. Trace the pattern onto the yellow poster board. Using the craft knife or sharp scissors, cut out the box.

2. To assemble the box, fold the side panels and triangular tabs in toward the center. Press firmly to make a sharp crease. Seal the side seam using the craft glue or hot glue gun. Allow to dry. For the bottom, fold the remaining tabs in toward the center. Press firmly to make a sharp crease. Seal the bottom seam using craft glue or the hot glue gun. Allow to dry.

Materials

- 1 sheet yellow poster board
- Box pattern (see page 63)
- Tracing paper
- Craft knife or sharp scissors
- Hot glue gun or all-purpose craft glue
- Assorted Easter stickers
- Multicolor cellophane or paper straw
- Six 2-inch plastic eggs
- $2/3$ yard of $1^1/_2$ - inch wide pink striped ribbon
- $2/3$ yard of $1^1/_2$ - inch wide yellow striped ribbon

3. Decorate the box with Easter stickers as desired. Fill the box with cellophane straw. Using a hot glue gun, attach three eggs along the base of each handle. Allow to dry.

4. To make the ribbons, insert one end of each ribbon through the box handles. Bring the ends together at the center. Tie them into a single knot. Trim as desired.

Wrapping Option

BASKETS ARE FOR EASTER.
When time is short, you can substitute a cheery basket for this handmade treat. Simply glue colorful plastic eggs around the rim of the basket and fill with straw as desired.

Full-size pattern

GHOSTS AND GOBLINS, page 49

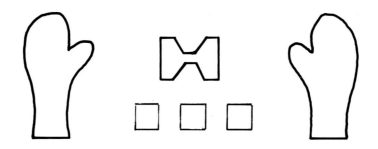

Full-size pattern

BLACK TIE BOTTLE, page 24

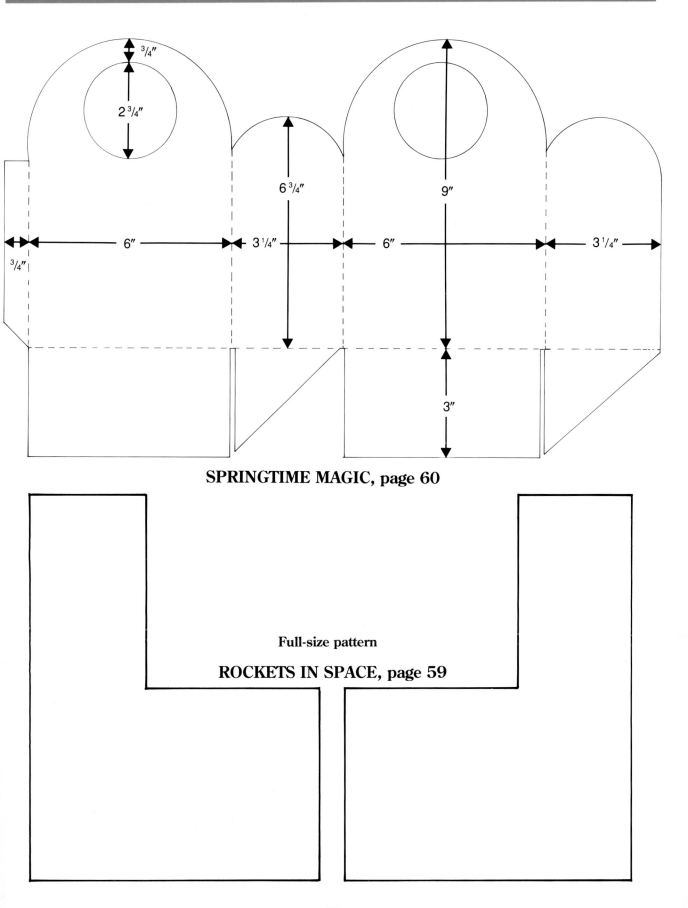

SPRINGTIME MAGIC, page 60

Full-size pattern

ROCKETS IN SPACE, page 59

TEMPLATES

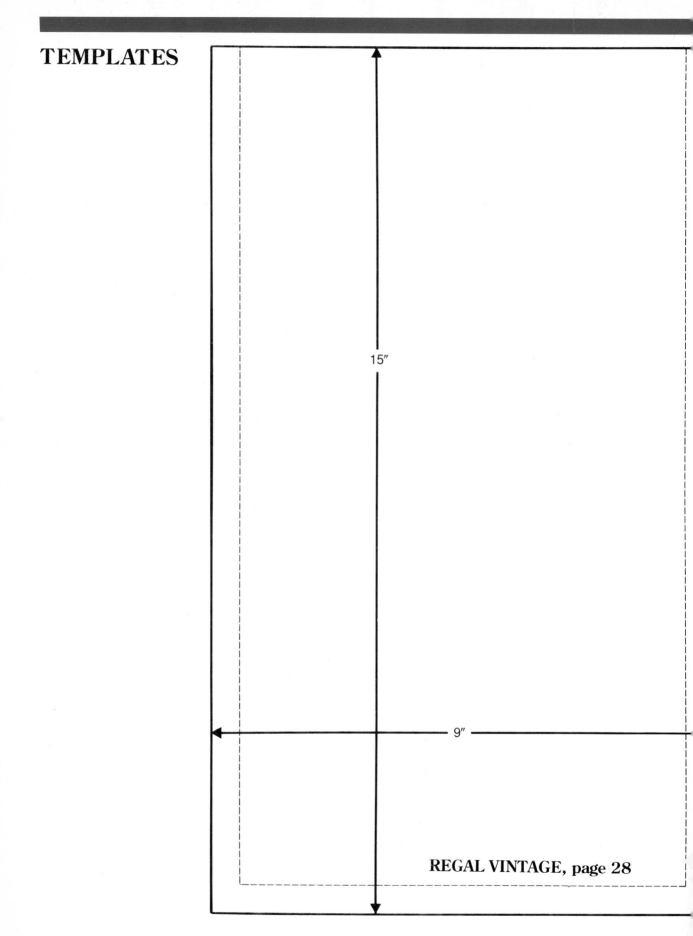

15″

9″

REGAL VINTAGE, page 28